WE ARE THE
GOALIES
The Top Netminders of the NHL

WE ARE THE GOALIES

THE TOP NETMINDERS OF THE NHL

CHRISTOPHER JORDAN

FENN
TUNDRA

INTRODUCTION

All NHL players share a passion for
hockey. From a young age, NHL
players committed themselves to
learning the sport and bettering their
skills. They worked hard to become
the very best.

The road to the NHL is a long one.
There are many young players chasing
a spot on a select team, looking to be
drafted — first in the bantam draft
and then the NHL. But being drafted
doesn't always mean an immediate
spot on an NHL roster. Many players
need to first prove their skills and
commitment in the minor leagues
and work hard to earn a chance to
play in the NHL. Once there, players

have to show up to every practice and every game with the right attitude and the determination to win. There will always be another player wanting that spot on the roster. Therefore, NHL players are the world's greatest hockey players. They are the players who, as young boys, led their teams, topped the minor leagues, and always played at the highest level of competition to show NHL scouts that they were ready for the big leagues. And they continue to play hard night after night, season after season.

We celebrate the game's very best in this book. These are the NHL's starting goalies.

JONAS HILLER

ANAHEIM DUCKS

NUMBER: 1
CATCHES: Right
HEIGHT: 6'2"
WEIGHT: 194 pounds
BIRTHDATE: February 12, 1982
BIRTHPLACE: Felben Wellhausen, Switzerland
SIGNED AS FREE AGENT: 2007 / Anaheim

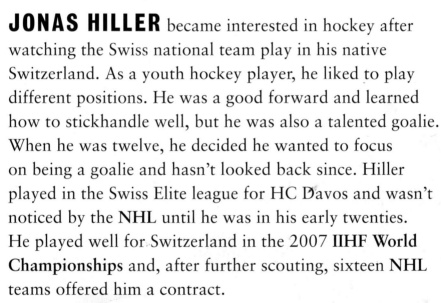

JONAS HILLER became interested in hockey after watching the Swiss national team play in his native Switzerland. As a youth hockey player, he liked to play different positions. He was a good forward and learned how to stickhandle well, but he was also a talented goalie. When he was twelve, he decided he wanted to focus on being a goalie and hasn't looked back since. Hiller played in the Swiss Elite league for HC Davos and wasn't noticed by the **NHL** until he was in his early twenties. He played well for Switzerland in the 2007 **IIHF World Championships** and, after further scouting, sixteen **NHL** teams offered him a contract.

Hiller spends his summers at goalie camp. He is known as a very hardworking netminder with a great **work ethic**. He is extremely flexible and **agile**. He moves quickly from one side of the goal **crease** to the other and covers much of the low part of his net by dropping his leg pads to the ice to block the puck.

TUUKKA RASK

BOSTON BRUINS

NUMBER: 40
CATCHES: Left
HEIGHT: 6'3"
WEIGHT: 169 pounds
BIRTHDATE: March 10, 1987
BIRTHPLACE: Savonlinna, Finland
DRAFTED: 2005 / Toronto (1st round / 21st overall)

TUUKKA RASK played junior hockey in the Finnish Junior League and was ranked the number-one goalie in Europe before the 2005 **NHL Entry Draft**. The Toronto Maple Leafs picked him twenty-first overall, but before he played a game with the Leafs, he was **traded** to Boston. Rask was the Bruins **starting goalie** at the beginning of the 2009–10 season. In 2010–11, he played in twenty-nine games for the Bruins and helped his team win the Stanley Cup championship that season.

Rask reads the play well. He has confidence and good reflexes. He plays the **butterfly style of goaltending**, with his knees close together so that he can quickly drop to the ice to stop the puck. Rask is a fast skater who can move in an instant across his net, **post to post**, to prevent a goal. He will often play at the top of the **crease** and challenge **shooters**. He has all the makings of a tremendous goalie.

RYAN MILLER

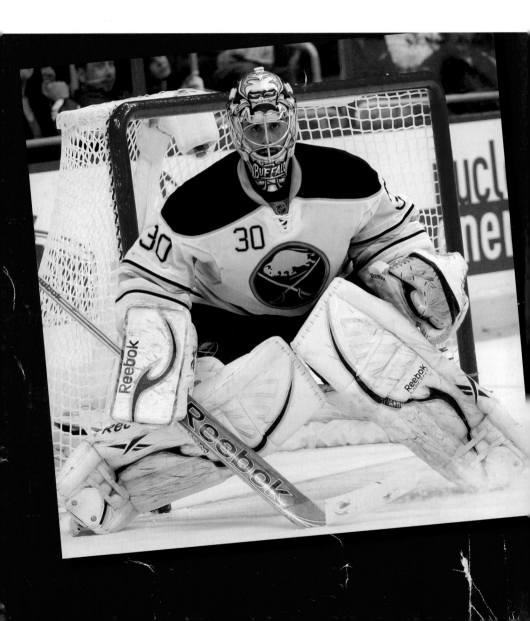

BUFFALO SABRES

NUMBER: 30
CATCHES: Left
HEIGHT: 6'2"
WEIGHT: 175 pounds
BIRTHDATE: July 17, 1980
BIRTHPLACE: East Lansing, Michigan, United States
DRAFTED: 1999 / Buffalo (5th round / 138th overall)

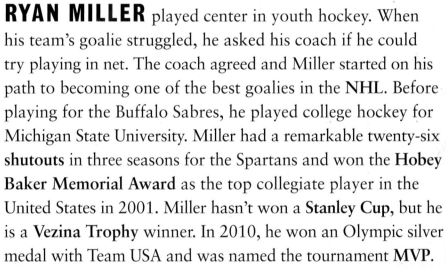

RYAN MILLER played center in youth hockey. When his team's goalie struggled, he asked his coach if he could try playing in net. The coach agreed and Miller started on his path to becoming one of the best goalies in the **NHL**. Before playing for the Buffalo Sabres, he played college hockey for Michigan State University. Miller had a remarkable twenty-six **shutouts** in three seasons for the Spartans and won the **Hobey Baker Memorial Award** as the top collegiate player in the United States in 2001. Miller hasn't won a **Stanley Cup,** but he is a **Vezina Trophy** winner. In 2010, he won an Olympic silver medal with Team USA and was named the tournament **MVP.**

Miller is an aggressive goalie who will leave his net to **poke-check** the puck away from an opponent. He is a **hybrid goalie** who **sees the puck well** and hugs his goalposts tightly to stop the puck from sneaking in. He has lightning-quick reflexes and can catch the puck out of the air with his glove or kick out his leg pad to stop the puck from crossing the **goal line.** Miller is a well-respected team leader.

MIIKKA KIPRUSOFF

CALGARY FLAMES

NUMBER: 34
CATCHES: Left
HEIGHT: 6'1"
WEIGHT: 185 pounds
BIRTHDATE: October 26, 1976
BIRTHPLACE: Turku, Finland
DRAFTED: 1995 / San Jose (5th round / 116th overall)

Before he reached the NHL, **MIIKKA KIPRUSOFF** played in Finland's elite league, the SM-liiga. In 1999, he was named the league's best goalie and the best player in the playoffs. He gained international experience playing for Finland at the **IIHF World Junior Championships** in 1995 and 1996 and played twice for Finland at the **IIHF World Championships** and the 2004 World Cup of Hockey. Kiprusoff was drafted by the San Jose Sharks and became a **starting goalie** when he was **traded** to the Calgary Flames. In his first season with the Flames, he helped lead his new team all the way to the **Stanley Cup** Final. He won the **Vezina Trophy** and the **William M. Jennings Trophy** in 2006.

Kiprusoff is a great team player. He is confident and **plays the puck** well. He knows where to position himself to best stop the puck and moves his arms and legs quickly to protect his net. He has a great **work ethic** and plays consistently night after night.

CAM WARD

CAROLINA HURRICANES

NUMBER: 35
CATCHES: Left
HEIGHT: 6'1"
WEIGHT: 185 pounds
BIRTHDATE: February 29, 1984
BIRTHPLACE: Saskatoon, Saskatchewan, Canada
DRAFTED: 2002 / Carolina (1st round / 25th overall)

CAM WARD played junior hockey in Alberta, and in his first season with the Red Deer Rebels, he won the **Bill Ranford Trophy**. He was selected twenty-fifth overall in the **NHL Entry Draft** by the Carolina Hurricanes. In his first **NHL** game, Ward faced two of the game's greatest players — Sidney Crosby and Mario Lemieux — in a shootout. He made great saves and stopped them both to help his team win the game. He was tested often in his first few games but showed that he was ready for the **NHL**. When the Hurricanes entered the playoffs that season, Ward's great goaltending helped them win their first **Stanley Cup** championship. He was voted playoff **MVP**, making him the first rookie goalie since Ron Hextall (in 1987) to win the **Conn Smythe Trophy**.

Like all good goalies, Ward is quick on his feet. He can get across the net in a flash to stop the puck, has a long reach with his **glove hand**, and does not give up big **rebounds**. He has a lot of confidence and it shows.

COREY CRAWFORD

CHICAGO BLACKHAWKS

NUMBER: 50
CATCHES: Left
HEIGHT: 6'2"
WEIGHT: 200 pounds
BIRTHDATE: December 31, 1984
BIRTHPLACE: Montreal, Quebec, Canada
DRAFTED: 2003 / Chicago (2nd round / 52nd overall)

Like so many of the **NHL**'s great goaltenders, **COREY CRAWFORD** played major junior hockey in the QMJHL. As a member of the Moncton Wildcats, he set a number of records that still stand. In 2005, he led the league with the best **goals-against average,** and in 2003–04 he won an incredible thirty-five games. No goalie for the club has matched that number of wins in a season since. Crawford was drafted by the Blackhawks and was the first Chicago goalie in over ten years to win at least thirty games in back-to-back seasons.

Crawford worked hard to earn the **starting goalie** role for the Blackhawks. He shows up for each game focused and ready to compete. He mostly plays the **butterfly style of goaltending,** and he covers the net quickly by dropping his leg pads to the ice to block the puck. Crawford is a great skater who **plays the puck** well. He tends to play deep in the **crease,** but he rarely gives up a costly **rebound.**

SEMYON VARLAMOV

COLORADO AVALANCHE

NUMBER: 1
CATCHES: Left
HEIGHT: 6'2"
WEIGHT: 209 pounds
BIRTHDATE: April 27, 1988
BIRTHPLACE: Samara, Russia
DRAFTED: 2006 / Washington (1st round / 23rd overall)

SEMYON VARLAMOV began playing goalie at the age of eight. Before entering the **NHL**, he played for Lokomotiv Yaroslavl, a team he helped lead to the 2008 finals of the Russian Superleague. He has played for Russia in several international tournaments, including the **IIHF World Junior Championships**, the **IIHF World Championships**, and the 2010 Winter Olympics. Varlamov was drafted by the Washington Capitals in 2006 and played his first **NHL** game in December 2008 against the Montreal Canadiens. He was named the **first star** of that game.

Varlamov plays the **butterfly style of goaltending**, dropping his leg pads to the ice quickly and snapping his **glove hand** out to catch the puck before it enters the net. He has a fast **blocker** and moves well in the **crease** to face **shooters**. He is a solid goalie with a tremendous future ahead of him.

SERGEI BOBROVSKY

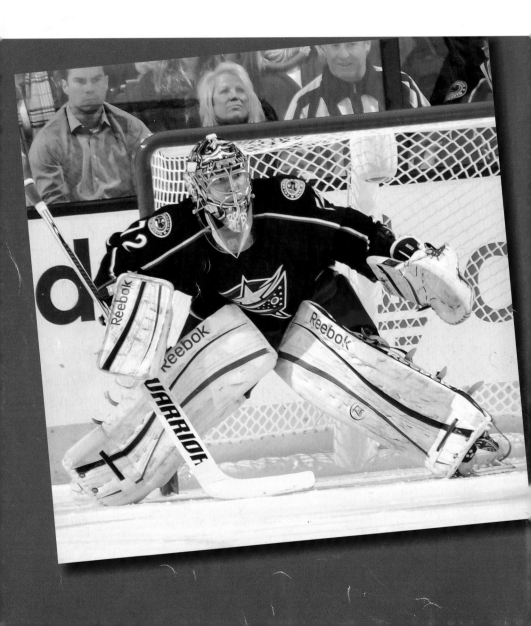

COLUMBUS BLUE JACKETS

NUMBER: 72
CATCHES: Left
HEIGHT: 6'2"
WEIGHT: 190 pounds
BIRTHDATE: September 20, 1988
BIRTHPLACE: Novokuznetsk, Russia
SIGNED AS FREE AGENT: 2012 / Philadelphia

SERGEI BOBROVSKY spent four seasons in Russia's Kontinental Hockey League. He put in solid performances each game and earned the starting goaltending position for Russia in the 2008 **IIHF World Junior Championship**. His **goals-against average** of 2.46 helped the Russians win the bronze medal. Bobrovsky was not drafted by an **NHL** team but was offered a contract by the Philadelphia Flyers. He was young and didn't have a lot of experience so it was expected that he would join their **farm team.** But after showing great strength at training camp, Bobrovsky earned the Flyer's backup spot and played fifty-four games during his rookie **NHL** season. He was traded to Columbus for the 2012–13 season and earned the starting role.

Bobrovsky can move across the **crease** with incredible speed. He has great vision of the ice and follows the play well. He plays a **butterfly style of goaltending.** Bobrovsky is a mature player and has a great **work ethic.**

KARI LEHTONEN

DALLAS STARS

NUMBER: 32
CATCHES: Left
HEIGHT: 6'4"
WEIGHT: 217 pounds
BIRTHDATE: November 16, 1983
BIRTHPLACE: Helsinki, Finland
DRAFTED: 2002 / Atlanta (1st round / 2nd overall)

KARI LEHTONEN's pre-NHL hockey career started in the Finnish league, the SM-liiga. Lehtonen was a very solid goalie for his team and had an incredible **goals-against average** of just 1.79 in 2001–02. As a result of his strong performance in 2001–02 and 2002–03, he won the Urpo Ylonen Trophy, presented to the league's best goalie. In 2002, he was awarded the Jari Kurri Trophy as the best goalie in the playoffs. His team won the championship that same season. He was picked second overall in the 2002 **NHL Entry Draft** by the Atlanta Thrashers, and he holds franchise records for most wins, most shutouts, and most games played by a goalie. In 2010, he was **traded** to the Dallas Stars.

Lehtonen plays a **butterfly style of goaltending**. He keeps his knees firmly together and gets his leg pads down to the ice quickly to block the puck. He **sees the ice well** and will recover to his feet quickly after stopping the first shot. He is flexible and an overall very strong goalie.

JIMMY HOWARD

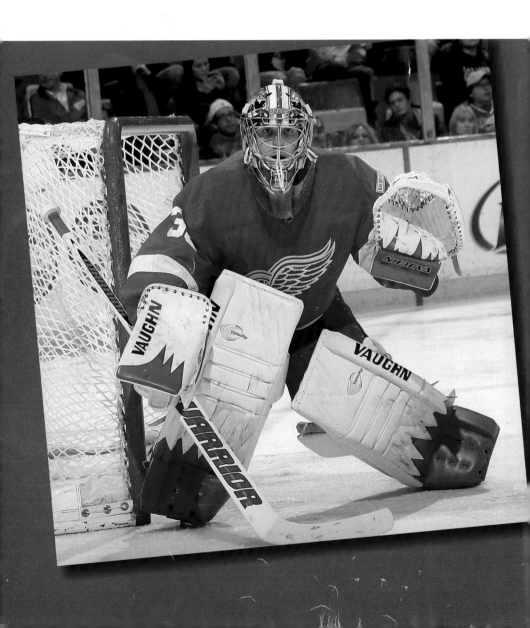

DETROIT RED WINGS

NUMBER: 35
CATCHES: Left
HEIGHT: 6'0"
WEIGHT: 218 pounds
BIRTHDATE: March 26, 1984
BIRTHPLACE: Syracuse, New York, United States
DRAFTED: 2003 / Detroit (2nd round / 64th overall)

JIMMY HOWARD played pre-NHL hockey at the University of Maine. His school competed in the Hockey East conference of the **NCAA**, and he still holds league records for **shutouts** and **goals-against average**. Howard was drafted by the Detroit Red Wings in 2003, but it wasn't until the 2009–10 season that he became the team's **starting goalie**. In his first full **NHL** season, he was the runner-up for the **Calder Memorial Trophy** and was selected to play in the **NHL All-Star Game** two years later.

Howard is a fun goalie to watch. He gets involved in the action and likes to **play the puck**. He **knows his angles** and covers his net well against all shooting positions. He is a strong skater and will often **poke-check** his opponents instead of waiting for them to shoot. The strong defense provided by his Detroit teammates helps him to play with great confidence.

DEVAN DUBNYK

EDMONTON OILERS

NUMBER: 40
CATCHES: Left
HEIGHT: 6'5"
WEIGHT: 210 pounds
BIRTHDATE: May 4, 1986
BIRTHPLACE: Regina, Saskatchewan, Canada
DRAFTED: 2004 / Edmonton (1st round / 14th overall)

DEVAN DUBNYK played junior hockey for the Kamloops Blazers of the **WHL**. In his last season with the team, he won the **Doc Seaman Memorial Trophy** as the top scholastic player. That same season, he also won the **CHL** Scholastic Player of the Year Award, given to the player who is best able to achieve success in school and hockey at the same time. Devan was selected fourteenth overall by the Edmonton Oilers in the first round of the 2004 **NHL Entry Draft,** and he was called up from the **minor leagues** to play as a **backup goalie** for the Oilers three seasons later. After playing well for his team, he earned the starting role.

Dubnyk's large size allows him to cover a lot of the net. He has quick reflexes and a great **glove hand**. He moves well from **post to post** and covers up **rebounds** well.

JOSE THEODORE

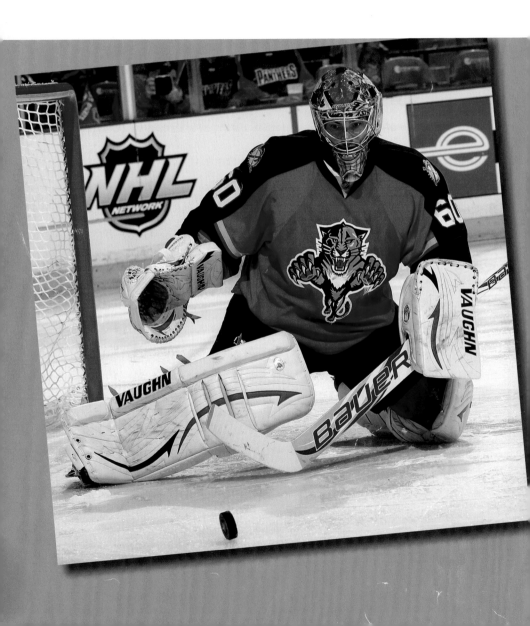

FLORIDA PANTHERS

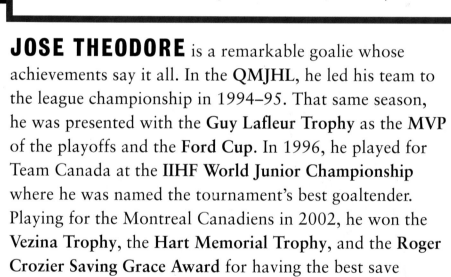

NUMBER: 60
CATCHES: Right
HEIGHT: 5'11"
WEIGHT: 172 pounds
BIRTHDATE: September 13, 1976
BIRTHPLACE: Laval, Quebec, Canada
DRAFTED: 1994 / Montreal (2nd round / 44th overall)

JOSE THEODORE is a remarkable goalie whose achievements say it all. In the **QMJHL**, he led his team to the league championship in 1994–95. That same season, he was presented with the **Guy Lafleur Trophy** as the **MVP** of the playoffs and the **Ford Cup**. In 1996, he played for Team Canada at the **IIHF World Junior Championship** where he was named the tournament's best goaltender. Playing for the Montreal Canadiens in 2002, he won the **Vezina Trophy**, the **Hart Memorial Trophy**, and the **Roger Crozier Saving Grace Award** for having the best save percentage in the **NHL**. In 2010, he was presented with the Bill Masterton Memorial Trophy for his exemplary sportsmanship and dedication to hockey.

Theodore handles pressure well. He has played in the **NHL** for many seasons and has a lot of playoff experience. He is a **butterfly-style goalie** who **knows his angles**. He has great side-to-side movement, and he quickly covers up **loose pucks** in the **crease**.

JONATHAN QUICK

LOS ANGELES KINGS

NUMBER: 32
CATCHES: Left
HEIGHT: 6'1"
WEIGHT: 201 pounds
BIRTHDATE: January 21, 1986
BIRTHPLACE: Milford, Connecticut, United States
DRAFTED: 2005 / Los Angeles (3rd round / 72nd overall)

JONATHAN QUICK was born in Connecticut and played youth hockey in his home state before following the **NCAA** route to the **NHL**. He attended the University of Massachusetts, where he was an important part of the hockey team. **NHL** scouts took notice of his goaltending skills. He was drafted by the L.A. Kings in 2005 and became the team's **starting goalie** at the beginning of the 2009–10 season.

When the Kings entered the 2012 playoffs, few thought they would go on to win **the Cup**. But Quick's heroic play in net helped his team capture the **Stanley Cup** championship. He was presented with the **Conn Smythe Trophy** as **MVP** of the playoffs. Quick is a great **butterfly-style goalie** and has terrific **post-to-post** speed. He will approach a **shooter** to cut down the angle of the shot, and he does not give up many **rebounds**.

NIKLAS BACKSTROM

MINNESOTA WILD

NUMBER: 32
CATCHES: Left
HEIGHT: 6'2"
WEIGHT: 194 pounds
BIRTHDATE: February 13, 1978
BIRTHPLACE: Helsinki, Finland
SIGNED AS FREE AGENT: 2006 / Minnesota

Before entering the NHL, **NIKLAS BACKSTROM** played in Finland's elite league, the SM-liiga. In 2003–04, he was named the Goalie of the Year and the Best Player of the Playoffs. He won both awards again in 2004–05. He has played for Finland at the **IIHF World Championship,** and he won a silver medal at the 2006 Olympics and a bronze at the 2010 Olympics. In his first **NHL** season, he had an incredible 1.97 **goals-against average,** the best of any goalie. He has won both the **William M. Jennings Trophy** and the **Roger Crozier Saving Grace Award.**

Backstrom has a lot of international playing experience. He is a **butterfly-style goalie** who shows up every night committed to win. He is fast on his skates and rarely gets beaten by low shots. Backstrom sees the ice well and anticipates the shot in time to position himself to stop it.

CAREY PRICE

MONTREAL CANADIENS

NUMBER: 31
CATCHES: Left
HEIGHT: 6'3"
WEIGHT: 219 pounds
BIRTHDATE: August 16, 1987
BIRTHPLACE: Anahim Lake, British Columbia, Canada
DRAFTED: 2005 / Montreal (1st round / 5th overall)

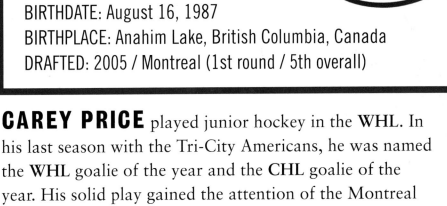

CAREY PRICE played junior hockey in the **WHL**. In his last season with the Tri-City Americans, he was named the **WHL** goalie of the year and the **CHL** goalie of the year. His solid play gained the attention of the Montreal Canadiens, who drafted him fifth overall in the 2005 **NHL Entry Draft**. Price joined the Canadiens' **AHL farm team**, the Hamilton Bulldogs, with only a few games left in their 2006–07 season. He led the team through the playoffs to the **Calder Cup** championship and was named the **MVP** of the playoffs.

Price has played in three **NHL All-Star Games**. He is a big goalie whose size allows him to naturally cover a lot of the net. He has great vision of the ice and reads the play well. He **knows his angles** and will play at the top of the **crease** so the **shooter** has less of the net to hit. He has a quick stick hand and **plays the puck** well.

PEKKA RINNE

NASHVILLE PREDATORS

NUMBER: 35
CATCHES: Left
HEIGHT: 6'5"
WEIGHT: 209 pounds
BIRTHDATE: November 3, 1982
BIRTHPLACE: Kempele, Finland
DRAFTED: 2004 / Nashville (8th round / 258th overall)

PEKKA RINNE is the one of the tallest goalies in the NHL. His height and size make him a very tough goalie to score on. He was born and raised in Finland and played in the SM-liiga for three seasons before the Nashville Predators drafted him in 2004. Rinne played with the Predators' **AHL farm team** before he got his chance to play in the **NHL** in 2008–09. He was called up to serve as a **backup goalie**, but before long, he took over the starting position and has not looked back. At the end of the 2011–12 season, he was a finalist for the **Vezina Trophy** and ended the year with more wins than any other **NHL** goalie.

Rinne is one of the most talented goalies in the **NHL**. He plays a unique style of **butterfly goaltending**, covering up the lower part of the net by quickly dropping to his knees to stop the puck, and then jumping back up on his skates to protect the net. He **plays the puck** well and can stop the puck on a shoot-in and pass it out quickly to a teammate. Rinne is an exciting goalie to watch!

MARTIN BRODEUR

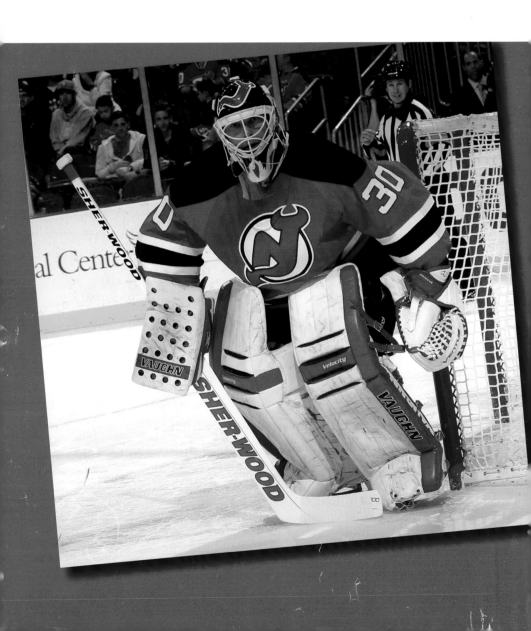

NEW JERSEY DEVILS

NUMBER: 30
CATCHES: Left
HEIGHT: 6'2"
WEIGHT: 220 pounds
BIRTHDATE: May 6, 1972
BIRTHPLACE: Montreal, Quebec, Canada
DRAFTED: 1990 / New Jersey (1st round / 20th overall)

In **MARTIN BRODEUR**'s first **NHL** season, he won the **Calder Memorial Trophy** as the league's best **rookie**. In his second season with the New Jersey Devils, he led them to their first **Stanley Cup** championship. Brodeur would go on to win the **Stanley Cup** again with New Jersey in 2000 and in 2003. He has competed for Canada internationally and captured Olympic gold in 2002 and 2010. He is a four-time **Vezina Trophy** winner, has played in ten **NHL All-Star Games**, and he has won the **William M. Jennings Trophy** five times.

Brodeur is considered by many to be the best goalie in **NHL** history. He has more wins than any other netminder and is one of only ten goalies who have ever scored a goal in an **NHL** game. He has amazing reflexes, and is difficult to deke because he does not easily get caught out of position. He reads the play well and **knows his angles** better than most. He is a good skater, has great **post-to-post** speed, and **plays the puck** extremely well. He is simply a sensational goalie.

EVGENI NABOKOV

NEW YORK ISLANDERS

NUMBER: 20
CATCHES: Left
HEIGHT: 6'0"
WEIGHT: 200 pounds
BIRTHDATE: July 25, 1975
BIRTHPLACE: Ust-Kamenogorsk, Kazakhstan
DRAFTED: 1994 / San Jose (9th round / 219th overall)

EVGENI NABOKOV was the first goalie from Kazakhstan to play in the **NHL**. He played youth hockey in his hometown, then moved to Moscow, Russia, to play for Dynamo Moscow of the Russian International Ice Hockey League. In his first season with Dynamo, Nabokov led his team to the championship and was named the **MVP**. Nabokov left for the **NHL** in 1997, signing with the San Jose Sharks. He played his first **NHL** game during the 1999–2000 season and earned a **shutout** by stopping each of the thirty-nine shots he faced. He played remarkably well in his first full season and won the **Calder Memorial Trophy** in 2001.

Nabokov has a lot of playing experience and is considered one of the **NHL's** best goalies. He has a lightning-fast **glove hand** that he uses to snag flying pucks out of midair. He uses the **butterfly style of goaltending** and can move across the **crease** very quickly. He **knows his angles** well and will take away any open net from the **shooter**.

HENRIK LUNDQVIST

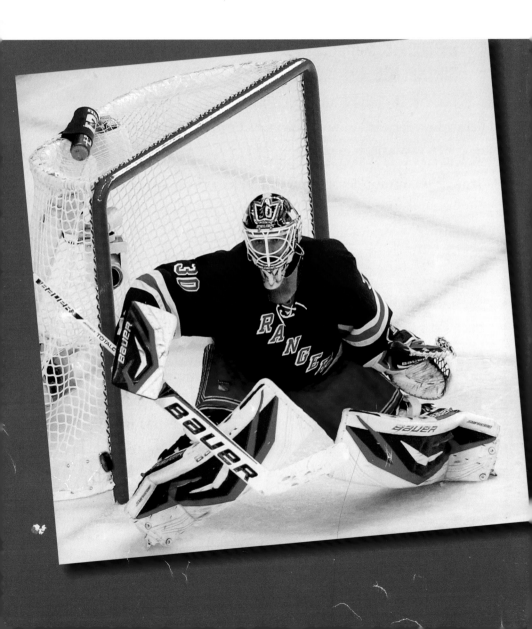

NEW YORK RANGERS

NUMBER: 30
CATCHES: Left
HEIGHT: 6'1"
WEIGHT: 195 pounds
BIRTHDATE: March 2, 1982
BIRTHPLACE: Are, Sweden
DRAFTED: 2000 / New York Rangers (7th round / 205th overall)

Before making his **NHL** debut, **HENRIK LUNDQVIST** played for Frolunda of the Swedish Elite League. Internationally, he has won two silver medals at the **IIHF World Championship** and an Olympic gold medal at the 2006 Winter Games. In his **rookie NHL** season with the New York Rangers, he was a finalist for the **Vezina Trophy,** a feat he repeated in his second season. He won the award in 2012. He has played in six **NHL All-Star Games** and has won thirty or more games in each of his seven **NHL** seasons.

Lundqvist is a **butterfly-style goalie.** He has a fast **glove hand,** and he can get his leg pads down to the ice instantly to stop the puck. He reads the play well and **knows his angles** better than most. He has great reflexes and moves from **post to post** with incredible speed. Lundqvist is strong in shootouts and plays well on breakaways.

CRAIG ANDERSON

OTTAWA SENATORS

NUMBER: 41
CATCHES: Left
HEIGHT: 6'2"
WEIGHT: 183 pounds
BIRTHDATE: May 21, 1981
BIRTHPLACE: Park Ridge, Illinois, United States
DRAFTED: 2001 / Chicago (3rd round / 73rd overall)

CRAIG ANDERSON played junior hockey in the OHL for the Guelph Storm. In 2001, he finished the season with a fantastic **goals-against average** and won the **OHL** Goaltender of the Year award. That same season, he was drafted by the Chicago Blackhawks. Anderson holds the **NHL** record for stopping the most shots in a **shutout** performance. Playing against the Islanders, he made fifty-three saves in a 1–0 win. He was **traded** to the Florida Panthers and later signed with the Colorado Avalanche as a **free agent**. He is now the **starting goalie** for the Ottawa Senators. Anderson has represented the United States internationally at two **IIHF World Championships**.

Anderson is a hardworking goalie who is committed to win. He makes spectacular saves and keeps his team in the game when the pressure is on. He has great reflexes, **sees the ice well,** and covers his corners.

ILYA BRYZGALOV

PHILADELPHIA FLYERS

NUMBER: 30
CATCHES: Left
HEIGHT: 6'3"
WEIGHT: 213 pounds
BIRTHDATE: June 22, 1980
BIRTHPLACE: Togliatti, Russia
DRAFTED: 2000 / Anaheim (2nd round / 44th overall)

Before playing in the NHL, **ILYA BRYZGALOV** played in the Russian Superleague. His competitiveness gained the attention of **NHL** scouts, and the Anaheim Ducks selected him in the 2000 **NHL Entry Draft.** Although Bryzgalov was the Ducks' **backup goaltender** during their 2006–07 **Stanley Cup** championship season, his performance in the first round of the playoffs helped Anaheim win. The Phoenix Coyotes grabbed him early in the 2007–08 season, and he had four great years with the Coyotes before being **traded** to the Philadelphia Flyers. With his new team, Bryzgalov became the **starting goalie** and set a club record for the longest **shutout** streak. He has won a gold medal at the **IIHF World Championship,** an Olympic bronze at the 2002 Winter Games, and a silver medal at the **IIHF World Junior Championship.**

Bryzgalov **plays the puck** well and **knows his angles.** He positions himself in the net for the best chance to see the **shooter** and stop the puck. He has quick arms and legs, and he gets himself in front of most shots.

MIKE SMITH

PHOENIX COYOTES

NUMBER: 41
CATCHES: Left
HEIGHT: 6'4"
WEIGHT: 218 pounds
BIRTHDATE: March 22, 1982
BIRTHPLACE: Kingston, Ontario, Canada
DRAFTED: 2001 / Dallas (5th round / 161st overall)

MIKE SMITH made his **OHL** debut in 1999–2000 for the Kingston Frontenacs, playing just eighteen games with the team before he was **traded** to the Sudbury Wolves. Smith was drafted by the Dallas Stars in the 2001 **NHL Entry Draft** and joined the team as their **backup goalie** for the 2006–07 season. After two years with Dallas, he was **traded** to the Tampa Bay Lightning. He spent four seasons with the Lightning and then signed with the Phoenix Coyotes for the start of the 2011–12 season. Smith played extremely well for his new team and led them deep into the 2012 playoffs.

Smith stands tall in the **crease** and protects his net well. He is a confident goalie who makes amazing saves by kicking out his legs quickly. He also has a very fast **glove hand** and has good vision of the ice. He **plays the puck** very well and helps his defense clear the zone with great shots.

MARC-ANDRE FLEURY

PITTSBURGH PENGUINS

NUMBER: 29
CATCHES: Left
HEIGHT: 6'2"
WEIGHT: 180 pounds
BIRTHDATE: November 28, 1984
BIRTHPLACE: Sorel, Quebec, Canada
DRAFTED: 2003 / Pittsburgh (1st round / 1st overall)

MARC-ANDRE FLEURY played junior hockey in the QMJHL, where he won the **Mike Bossy Trophy** in 2003 as the league's top **prospect**. That same year he was the **first-overall** pick in the **NHL Entry Draft**. He made his **NHL** debut the next fall at just eighteen years old. In his first game for the Penguins, he made forty-six amazing saves against the Los Angeles Kings. Fleury became Pittsburgh's **starting goalie** for the 2005–06 season. In 2009, Fleury's remarkable goaltending skills helped his team win the **Stanley Cup** and earned him an invitation to **Hockey Canada's training camp** and ultimately a place on Canada's 2010 Olympic team.

Fleury is an excellent goalie. He is tall and lean and can move across the net quickly. He plays the **butterfly style of goaltending** and drops his leg pads to the ice fast to stop the puck. He has great focus and makes important saves to help his team. Fleury has a lot of valuable playoff experience.

ANTTI NIEMI

SAN JOSE SHARKS

NUMBER: 31
CATCHES: Left
HEIGHT: 6'2"
WEIGHT: 210 pounds
BIRTHDATE: August 29, 1983
BIRTHPLACE: Vantaa, Finland
SIGNED AS FREE AGENT: 2008 / Chicago

Originally from Finland, **ANTTI NIEMI** moved to the **NHL** in 2008 as a **free agent**. As the **starting goalie** for the Chicago Blackhawks, he led his team with amazing goaltending through all four rounds of the 2010 playoffs to capture the **Stanley Cup**. In the next two seasons, Niemi started in net for the San Jose Sharks and won over thirty games in back-to-back seasons.

Niemi is an experienced goalie. He does not allow a bad goal to rattle him and can maintain focus even in tense, close games. He has great flexibility and moves as quick as a cat to get across the **crease** to stop a shot. He is an exciting goalie to watch as he uses all of his body and equipment to protect his net.

JAROSLAV HALAK

ST. LOUIS BLUES

NUMBER: 41
CATCHES: Left
HEIGHT: 5'11"
WEIGHT: 182 pounds
BIRTHDATE: May 13, 1985
BIRTHPLACE: Bratislava, Slovakia
DRAFTED: 2003 / Montreal (9th round / 271st overall)

The Montreal Canadiens picked **JAROSLAV HALAK** late in the 2003 **NHL Entry Draft** on the strength of his play in the junior ranks in his native Slovakia. He later played in his home country's top league, the Extraliga, and in the **QMJHL** and **AHL**. In 2006–07, Halak finally got his chance to play in the **NHL** when the Canadiens called him up. He won his first **NHL** game and earned his chance to stay in the league. Halak spent the next two seasons as the Canadiens' **backup goalie,** and by the end of the 2009–10 season, he had been named the team's **starting goalie.** Halak's play during the 2010 playoffs earned him the Molson Cup as the Canadiens' player of the year. Halak was **traded** to the St. Louis Blues and ended the 2011–12 season with an amazing **goals-against average** of 1.97.

Halak is a hardworking goalie who has good on-ice vision. He plays well in shootouts and knows how to control **rebounds.** He can stop a lot of shots without losing focus and is a good team player.

ANDERS LINDBACK

TAMPA BAY LIGHTNING

NUMBER: 39
CATCHES: Left
HEIGHT: 6'6"
WEIGHT: 203 pounds
BIRTHDATE: May 3, 1988
BIRTHPLACE: Gavle, Sweden
DRAFTED: 2008 / Nashville (7th round / 207th overall)

ANDERS LINDBACK arrived in the **NHL** after playing well in Sweden's two highest ranking professional hockey leagues — the Elitserien and Almtuna IS, Uppsala. Lindback was drafted by the Nashville Predators in 2008, and he became the club's **backup goalie** for the 2010–11 season. Lindback worked hard with the coaching staff and his teammates to improve his skills. In his first **NHL** season, he started in twenty-two games and ended the year with a **goals-against average** of 2.60. Lindback was involved in a multi-player **trade** at the end of the 2012 season. He became the starting goalie for the Tampa Bay Lightning at the beginning of the 2013 season.

Lindback plays a **hybrid** style of goaltending. He often frustrates **shooters** by stopping pucks that would get by many other goalies. His impressive size allows him to cover up a great deal of the net. Lindback is a young goalie with the passion to win and an incredible **work ethic**.

JAMES REIMER

TORONTO MAPLE LEAFS

NUMBER: 34
CATCHES: Left
HEIGHT: 6'2"
WEIGHT: 208 pounds
BIRTHDATE: March 15, 1988
BIRTHPLACE: Morweena, Manitoba, Canada
DRAFTED: 2006 / Toronto (4th round / 99th overall)

While most Canadian boys register for tyke hockey at the age of five, **JAMES REIMER** didn't play organized youth hockey until he was twelve. Even so, an agent took note of his skills when he was just thirteen, and two years later, in 2003, he was picked in the **WHL** bantam draft. In 2006, the Toronto Maple Leafs selected him in the **NHL Entry Draft,** and by the 2010–11 season, he was playing backup for the Leafs in the **NHL**. He played well in his **rookie** season and was invited to play for Team Canada at the 2011 **IIHF World Championship**. He ended the series with a 2.04 **goals-against average.**

Reimer is a **butterfly-style goalie.** He **plays the puck** well, **knows his angles,** and positions himself at the edge of the **crease** to face the **shooter.** He has good **post-to-post** speed and plays with tremendous focus. Reimer has good control of **rebounds** and covers up **loose pucks** quickly.

ROBERTO LUONGO

VANCOUVER CANUCKS

NUMBER: 1
CATCHES: Left
HEIGHT: 6'3"
WEIGHT: 217 pounds
BIRTHDATE: April 4, 1979
BIRTHPLACE: Montreal, Quebec, Canada
DRAFTED: 1997 / New York Islanders (1st round / 4th overall)

ROBERTO LUONGO played junior hockey in Quebec. In his last season in the **QMJHL**, he won the **Mike Bossy Trophy** as the top **prospect** heading into the 1997 **NHL Entry Draft**. Drafted by the Islanders, he played one season with New York before being **traded** to the Florida Panthers and then to the Vancouver Canucks. He has recorded sixty career **shutouts**. He has played in the **NHL All-Star Game** four times and won the **William M. Jennings Trophy,** and been a finalist for the **Vezina Trophy**. Luongo has played for Canada at the **IIHF World Junior Championship**, the World Cup of Hockey, and the **IIHF World Championship**. He stood tall for Team Canada at the 2010 Winter Olympics and was a big part of the team's gold medal win.

Luongo plays the **butterfly style of goaltending**. He is a big man who covers a lot of the net. He has quick reflexes and positions himself well in his net. He **plays the puck** and covers up **rebounds** well. He has a great **glove hand** and is tough to beat on that side of the net.

BRADEN HOLTBY

WASHINGTON CAPITALS

NUMBER: 70
CATCHES: Left
HEIGHT: 6'2"
WEIGHT: 203 pounds
BIRTHDATE: September 16, 1989
BIRTHPLACE: Lloydminster, Saskatchewan, Canada
DRAFTED: 2008 / Washington (4th round / 93rd overall)

BRADEN HOLTBY played junior hockey in the WHL for the Saskatoon Blades and was rated the number-four junior goalie in North America going into the 2008 **NHL Entry Draft**. He played in fourteen games in 2010–11, winning ten and finishing the year with a 1.79 **goals-against average**. During the 2012 playoffs, he was named the Capitals' **starting goalie** and played very well.

Holtby plays a **butterfly style of goaltending**. He is a great athlete who can drop to his knees and get back up on his skates quickly. He plays with great enthusiasm, and he has a very good **work ethic**. Holtby plays with a high level of energy, amazing reflexes, and a very quick **glove hand**. He **plays the puck** well and with confidence.

ONDREJ PAVELEC

WINNIPEG JETS

NUMBER: 31
CATCHES: Left
HEIGHT: 6'3"
WEIGHT: 220 pounds
BIRTHDATE: August 31, 1987
BIRTHPLACE: Kladno, Czech Republic
DRAFTED: 2005 / Atlanta (2nd round / 41st overall)

ONDREJ PAVELEC began playing hockey as a young boy in the Czech Republic. He then played junior hockey in the **QMJHL**, where he showed a consistent level of skill in two seasons with the Cape Breton Screaming Eagles, posting the best **goals-against average** in the league and winning the **Jacques Plante Memorial Trophy** both years. He has represented his home country at the **IIHF World Junior Championship,** twice at the **IIHF World Championship,** and at the 2010 Olympics. Pavelec was drafted by the Atlanta Thrashers and became the Winnipeg Jets' **starting goalie** at the beginning of the 2011–12 season when the team moved to Canada.

Pavelec is a big goalie who uses his size to cover up as much of the net as possible. He has a tremendous **work ethic** and plays with enthusiasm every game. He is a good athlete who plays the **butterfly style of goaltending** well.

GLOSSARY OF HOCKEY TERMS

agile: able to move quickly and with great flexibility

AHL: American Hockey League

backup goalie: a team's second goalie

Bill Ranford Trophy: award presented to the best goalie in the Alberta Midget Hockey League

blocker: goalie glove worn on the hand that holds the stick; also used to block the puck

butterfly style of goaltending: style of play where the goalie stands with his feet wide apart and his knees together, allowing him to quickly drop to the ice to protect the lower part of the net

Calder Cup: American Hockey League championship trophy

Calder Memorial Trophy: award presented to the NHL Rookie of the Year

CHL: Canadian Hockey League

Conn Smythe Trophy: award presented to the most valuable player in the Stanley Cup playoffs

crease: area of ice (painted blue) directly in front of the goal net

Doc Seaman Memorial Trophy: award presented to the top scholastic player in the WHL

farm team: minor league team connected to an NHL club, whose job is to develop players for the NHL

first overall: the player chosen in the NHL Entry Draft ahead of all others; usually the player thought to be the best among those available

first star: top player in a game

Ford Cup: trophy presented annually to the top defensive player in the QMJHL

free agent: player who is not under contract to any team

glove hand: goalie's catching hand

goal line: red line on the ice that stretches from one goalpost to the other; the puck must cross this line to be a goal

goals-against average (GAA): statistic that indicates how many goals a goalie allows per sixty minutes played

Guy Lafleur Trophy: award presented to the MVP of the QMJHL playoffs

Hart Memorial Trophy: award presented by the NHL to its most valuable player

Hobey Baker Memorial Award: trophy presented to the best player in U.S. collegiate hockey

Hockey Canada's training camp: series of practices held to determine which players will play on Canada's national teams; once the teams are chosen, the players practice and prepare for upcoming tournaments

hybrid goalie: goalie who plays both the butterfly and traditional style of goaltending

IIHF: International Ice Hockey Federation

IIHF World Championship: annual international hockey tournament where member countries of the IIHF compete

IIHF World Junior Championship: annual international hockey tournament between member countries of the IIHF, at which all players must be younger than twenty to compete

Jacques Plante Memorial Trophy: award presented annually to the goaltender in the QMJHL with the best goals-against average

knows his angles: being aware of where to position yourself to give an opponent the poorest view of the net, thereby preventing him from taking a good shot

Lester B. Pearson Award: trophy presented by the NHLPA to the player its members judge to be the most valuable in the regular season (now known as the Ted Lindsay Award)

loose puck: puck not under the control of either team

Mike Bossy Trophy: award presented to the best professional prospect in the QMJHL, among players eligible for the NHL Entry Draft

minor league: a professional league that is a level below the NHL

MVP: most valuable player

NCAA: National Collegiate Athletic Association

NHL: National Hockey League

NHL All-Star Game: an annual game in which the NHL's best players are invited to compete

NHL Entry Draft: an annual event at which each NHL team chooses players aged eighteen and up who do not already belong to an NHL club

OHL: Ontario Hockey League

play the puck: using the goal stick to pass the puck to a teammate, or stop the puck as it travels around the boards behind the net

poke check: use of the goal stick to knock the puck off an opponent's stick to prevent him from shooting

post to post: movement from one side of the net to the other

prospect: junior hockey player under consideration by NHL teams

QMJHL: Quebec Major Junior Hockey League

rebound: a puck that bounces off of the goalie's equipment and remains an active, loose puck and in play

Roger Crozier Saving Grace Award: award that was once presented to the NHL goalie with the best save percentage

rookie: player in his first NHL season

see the ice well: to know where other players and the puck are, and how plays are developing, at all times

see the puck well: to know where the puck is and where it is going

shooter: puck carrier who is planning to shoot on goal

shutout: game in which the goalie does not allow a single goal

Stanley Cup: NHL championship trophy

starting goalie: goalie who plays the majority of games for his team

trade: transfer of a player from one team to another, in exchange for another player, draft choices, or cash

Vezina Trophy: award presented annually to the NHL's best goalie

WHL: Western Hockey League

William M. Jennings Trophy: award presented to the goalie(s) on the NHL team that allows the fewest goals in the regular season

work ethic: belief in working very hard for your team